SHE GOVERNS AND AT THE HELM

STRATEGIES FOR POLITICAL EMPOWERMENT

DR. MINAKSHI BANSAL

DEDICATION

To the trailblazers, the glass-ceiling shatterers, and the changemakers.

To the women who dare to lead, who speak their truth, and who fight for a more just and equitable world.

To the next generation of women leaders, may your voices be heard, your dreams realized, and your impact felt across the globe.

ϷϷϷ

Contents

Contents

Prayer

"Om Bhadram Karnebhih Shrinuyama Devah

Bhadram Pashyemakshabhiryajatrah

Sthirairangais Tushtuvamsastanubhih

Vyashema Devahitam Yadayuh

Svasti Na Indro Vriddhashravah

Svasti Nah Pusha Vishwavedah

Svasti Nastarkshyo Arishtanemih

Svasti No Brihaspatir Dadhatu

Om Shantih Shantih Shantih"

This mantra is a prayer for universal well-being, invoking the blessings of various deities for protection, health, and happiness. It emphasizes the importance of experiencing the auspicious through all senses and living a life aligned with divine purpose. The repetition of "Shantih" at the end signifies a deep desire for peace in the individual, the environment, and the universe at large. This mantra is often recited as a prayer for peace, prosperity, and the physical and spiritual well-being of all beings.

About The Author

This book represents the culmination of extensive research and meticulous analysis, incorporating a diverse range of sources, including numerous books, scholarly studies, and personal experiences. Additionally, I have scoured various websites to gather relevant information and data essential for the compilation of this work. I have taken every precaution to ensure the accuracy of the information presented and have diligently cited all sources to acknowledge their contributions.

From her earliest days, Minakshi was distinguished by an insatiable appetite for reading. Her literary universe was inhabited by characters and narratives that spanned ethical tales, motivational and inspirational stories, and the mythic parables imbued with life lessons. This voracious reading habit was not merely for personal edification but was driven by a desire to distill and disseminate the essence of these narratives to foster the development of students and peers alike. She was particularly captivated by the lives and teachings of historical figures and spiritual leaders such as Adi Shankaracharya, Swami Vivekananda, Dr. APJ Abdul Kalam, Mahamana Pandit Madan Mohan Malviya, Mahatma Gandhi, Sardar Vallabhai Patel, and Vinoba Bhave, among others. Their philosophies and life stories fueled her ambition to embody their ideals of resilience, selflessness, and relentless pursuit of knowledge.

Dr. Minakshi's academic and practical engagement with psychology has been equally noteworthy. As a research scholar, her focus has been on exploring the intricate tapestry of the human psyche, aiming to unlock the potential for psychological well-being and societal harmony. Her scholarly work is complemented by her active involvement in social work, where she employs her academic insights to make tangible differences in the lives of the underprivileged. Her endeavours in social work are characterized by an innovative approach that combines traditional wisdom with contemporary psychological practices to address the multifaceted challenges faced by these communities.

Her artistic talents, another facet of her diverse capabilities, are not merely a personal passion but also serve as a medium through which she communicates and connects with others. Her art, rich in symbolism and emotional depth, reflects her philosophical inquiries and social concerns, offering viewers a glimpse into the breadth of her intellect and the depth of her compassion.

In addition to her contributions to the arts and social sciences, Dr. Minakshi has embraced the healing arts of Pranic Healing, mastering the techniques developed by Master Choa Kok Sui. This practice, which focuses on the manipulation of Prana or life energy to heal the body and aura, has been both a personal journey of discovery and a means through which she extends her healing touch to others. Her proficiency in Pranic Healing is complemented by her advocacy and teaching of various forms of meditation aimed at rejuvenation, personal betterment, and the cultivation of harmony within individuals and communities alike.

Dr. Minakshi's life is a narrative of relentless pursuit, not just of personal achievement but of the upliftment and empowerment of society at large. Her diverse interests and talents—spanning the arts, literature, psychology, and the healing practices—converge on a singular path of service. She embodies the spirit of the luminaries who inspired her, channelling their legacy through her actions and teachings. Through her books, art, and social initiatives, she continues to inspire a new generation to embark on their own journeys of self-discovery, resilience, and altruism.

Her commitment to social betterment, particularly her focus on uplifting underprivileged children, reflects a deep understanding of the transformative potential of education and personal development. By integrating her knowledge of psychology, her artistic sensibilities, and her healing practices, Dr. Bansal has developed a holistic approach to social work that addresses both the immediate needs and the long-term well-being of the communities she serves.

As an author, Dr. Minakshi's writings offer a blend of inspirational insights, practical wisdom, and reflective contemplations drawn from her extensive reading and life experiences. Her books serve as a guide for those seeking to navigate the complexities of life with grace, resilience, and purpose. Through her narratives, she extends an invitation to her readers to explore the depths of their own potential and to contribute meaningfully to the collective well-being of society.

In Dr. Minakshi Bansal, we find a remarkable synthesis of the artist, the scholar, the healer, and the social activist. Her life's work stands as a beacon of hope and a source of inspiration for individuals seeking to make a difference in the world. Her story is a compelling reminder of the power of individual action, rooted in compassion and driven by a profound commitment to the betterment of humanity. Dr. Minakshi's legacy is not just in the tangible outcomes of her efforts but in the enduring spirit of inquiry, empathy, and service that she embodies.

ととと

Preface

In a world where power dynamics are constantly shifting, the pursuit of political empowerment for women remains a critical endeavor.

This book, born from a deep-seated belief in the transformative power of women's leadership, is a testament to the resilience, ingenuity, and unwavering determination of women who have dared to challenge the status quo and reshape the political landscape.

This book is not just a collection of strategies; it's a call to action, a rallying cry for women to embrace their agency, amplify their voices, and claim their rightful place at the helm of power. It's a guide for navigating the complexities of the political arena, overcoming obstacles, and building a movement for change.

The impetus for this work stems from a profound recognition of the unique challenges and biases that women face in politics. From systemic barriers to ingrained stereotypes, the path to political leadership is often fraught with obstacles that can deter even the most ambitious and talented women.

However, history is replete with examples of women who have defied the odds, shattered glass ceilings, and emerged as transformative leaders.

This book seeks to amplify those stories, to celebrate the achievements of women who have paved the way, and to inspire a new generation of women leaders to rise to the challenge. It's a testament to the power of women's voices, the strength of their networks, and the impact of their collective action.

Within these pages, you will find a wealth of insights, strategies, and practical tools for navigating the political landscape. We will explore the importance of finding your political voice, building strong networks, mastering the art of persuasion, and navigating complex political structures.

We will delve into the intricacies of fundraising, crafting winning messages, and mastering public speaking. We will examine the role of the media, the power of collaboration, and the importance of mentoring the next generation.

This book is not just for women who aspire to hold political office. It's for all women who want to make a difference in their communities, advocate for change, and shape the future. It's for activists, organizers, educators, and anyone who believes in the transformative power of women's leadership.

The strategies outlined in this book are not a one-size-fits-all solution. They are meant to be adapted and applied to the unique circumstances and challenges faced by women in different contexts.

The goal is not to provide a prescriptive formula for success but to empower women with the knowledge, skills, and confidence to chart their own path to political empowerment.

This book is also a call for solidarity and collective action. The challenges facing women in politics are not individual problems; they are systemic issues that require a collective response.

By working together, supporting each other, and building a movement for change, we can create a more inclusive and equitable political system where women's voices are heard, their contributions are valued, and their leadership is celebrated.

The journey to political empowerment is not an easy one, but it is a necessary one. The stakes are high, the challenges are real, but the rewards are immeasurable.

By embracing our power, amplifying our voices, and working together, we can create a world where women not only govern but also lead the way in building a more just and equitable society for all.

Dr. Minakshi Bansal
Social Activist
Ahmedabad, Gujarat, Bharat

ONE
FINDING YOUR POLITICAL VOICE

Finding your political voice is not a singular event, but a lifelong journey. It begins with self-reflection, understanding your passions, values, and the change you want to see in the world. Your voice is unique, shaped by your experiences, identity, and the communities you belong to. It's the core of your political identity, the compass that guides your actions and decisions.

The first step is recognizing that your voice matters. Every individual, regardless of background or experience, has the right to participate in the political process. Your perspective is valuable, and your opinions have the power to influence decisions that affect your life and the lives of others. Don't underestimate the impact of your voice, even if it seems small at first.

Identifying your passions is crucial. What issues resonate with you deeply? What injustices make you angry or inspire you to action? Your passions are the fuel that will sustain you through the challenges of political engagement. They will motivate you to learn more, speak out, and work towards solutions. By focusing on issues you care about, you'll find your voice becoming stronger and more authentic.

Your values are the guiding principles that shape your worldview and political beliefs. They are the moral compass that helps you make ethical choices and stand up for what you believe in. By understanding your values, you can articulate your positions with clarity and conviction. When your actions align with your values, your voice becomes more powerful and persuasive.

Connecting with your community is essential for finding your political voice. Surround yourself with people who share your passions and values. Engage in conversations, attend meetings, and participate in events where you can learn from others and exchange ideas. By building relationships and finding common ground, you'll discover your voice resonating with a wider audience.

Education is key to developing your political voice. Learn about the issues that matter to you, research different perspectives, and understand the complexities of the political system. The more informed you are, the more confident you'll become in expressing your opinions and advocating for change. Seek out reliable sources of information, challenge your assumptions, and be open to new ideas.

Speaking out is a powerful way to find your voice. Share your opinions with friends, family, and colleagues. Write letters to your elected officials, participate in public forums, and use social media to amplify your message. Don't be afraid to voice your dissent or challenge the status quo. The more you practice speaking out, the stronger your voice will become.

Taking action is essential for turning your voice into real-world impact. Volunteer for campaigns, join advocacy groups, or run for office yourself. By getting involved, you can directly influence policy decisions and make a difference in your community. Even small actions, like attending a rally or contacting your representatives, can have a ripple effect.

Don't be discouraged by setbacks or opposition. The political arena can be challenging, but your voice is worth fighting for. Remember that progress is often slow and incremental. Celebrate small victories, learn from mistakes, and never give up on your vision for a better future.

Finding your political voice is not a solo endeavor. Seek out mentors and role models who can guide you and offer support. Build alliances with like-minded individuals and organizations. By working together, you can amplify your collective voices and create lasting change.

Remember, your political voice is a powerful tool for shaping the world around you. Embrace it, nurture it, and use it to advocate for the change you want to see. Your voice matters, and your participation in the political process is essential for building a more just and equitable society.

ᐅᐅᐅ

"Persuasion is an art, a dance of words and emotions. Connect with your audience on a deeper level, speak to their hearts, and ignite their passion for a better future. In the symphony of politics, your message is the melody that moves hearts and minds."

TWO

BUILDING NETWORKS: POWER IN NUMBERS

The adage "There is strength in numbers" is a profound truth, especially for women in the political arena. The journey towards empowerment is not one to be taken alone. It's a collective endeavor, a symphony of voices harmonizing to create lasting change. Building networks is not merely about socializing; it's a strategic imperative for amplifying our influence and achieving our goals.

As women, we often face unique challenges and biases in the political sphere. We may encounter systemic barriers, stereotypes, and a lack of representation in decision-making roles. Building strong networks helps us overcome these obstacles by providing support, mentorship, and solidarity. It creates a safe space where we can share experiences, learn from each other, and develop the skills necessary to thrive in the political landscape.

Networking is not about accumulating contacts; it's about cultivating genuine relationships built on trust, respect, and shared values. It's about finding allies who share our passion for gender equality and social justice. These connections can be invaluable sources of information, advice, and opportunities. They can open doors that may otherwise remain closed and provide a platform for our voices to be heard.

The power of networks lies in their ability to amplify our individual efforts. When we join forces with like-minded women, our collective impact is far greater than the sum of our individual contributions. We can pool our resources, leverage our expertise, and mobilize our supporters to achieve common goals. By working together, we can create a movement for change that is unstoppable.

There are various types of networks we can build to enhance our political power. Professional networks connect us with women in similar fields, providing opportunities for mentorship, collaboration, and career advancement. Political networks introduce us to elected officials, activists, and organizations working on issues we care about. Community networks connect us with women in our neighborhoods, schools, and workplaces, creating a grassroots movement for change.

Social media has revolutionized the way we build networks. It provides a platform for connecting with women from all walks of life, regardless of geographic location or background. Online communities can be powerful sources of support, information, and inspiration. They can also be used to mobilize supporters, raise awareness about important issues, and advocate for policy change.

Attending conferences, workshops, and other events focused on women's empowerment is another effective way to build networks. These gatherings provide opportunities to meet influential women, learn about new initiatives, and connect with potential mentors and collaborators. They can also be a source of inspiration and motivation, reminding us that we are not alone in our pursuit of equality.

Mentorship is a crucial aspect of building networks. A mentor can provide guidance, support, and encouragement as we navigate the challenges of political engagement. They can share their experiences, offer advice, and open doors to new opportunities. By seeking out mentors and offering mentorship to others, we can create a virtuous cycle of empowerment.

Collaboration is key to maximizing the impact of our networks. By working together, we can achieve far more than we could alone. We can share resources, expertise, and connections to create comprehensive solutions to complex problems. Collaboration also fosters a sense of community and shared purpose, which can be a powerful motivator for sustained action.

Building networks is not a one-time event; it's an ongoing process. It requires effort, intentionality, and a willingness to invest in relationships. By cultivating genuine connections with other women, we can create a powerful network that amplifies our voices, strengthens our influence, and empowers us to create lasting change.

Remember, the power of numbers is on our side. By building strong networks, we can create a movement for women's empowerment that is unstoppable. Let us join forces, lift each other up, and work together to create a more just and equitable world for all.

ppp

"The political landscape is a complex maze, but with knowledge and strategy, you can navigate its twists and turns. Understand the rules of the game, build alliances, and use your influence to create lasting change. Remember, knowledge is power, and power is the key to transformation."

THREE

THE ART OF PERSUASION AND INFLUENCE

The art of persuasion and influence is not merely a tool for manipulation; it's a fundamental skill for effective leadership and advocacy. For women in politics, mastering this art is essential for navigating the complexities of the political landscape, building coalitions, and driving meaningful change. It's about inspiring others to share our vision, mobilizing support for our initiatives, and ultimately, making a difference in the world.

At its core, persuasion is about understanding and connecting with people on a deep level. It's about recognizing their needs, values, and aspirations, and tailoring our message to resonate with their individual perspectives. It's not about imposing our views on others, but rather, about inviting them to see the world through our eyes and share our passion for a better future.

The first step in mastering persuasion is developing a deep understanding of our audience. Who are we trying to reach? What are their concerns, interests, and motivations? By putting ourselves in their shoes and seeing the world from their perspective, we can craft messages that speak directly to their hearts and minds.

Once we understand our audience, we can tailor our message to resonate with their values and beliefs. This doesn't mean compromising our principles or watering down our message. It means framing our arguments in a way that makes sense to our audience and aligns with their worldview. By highlighting shared values and common ground, we can build bridges of understanding and create a foundation for collaboration.

Storytelling is a powerful tool for persuasion. By sharing personal anecdotes, case studies, and real-life examples, we can make our message more relatable and engaging. Stories have the power to evoke emotions, create connections, and inspire action. They can also help us break down complex issues into simple, understandable terms.

Effective communication is essential for persuasion. We need to be clear, concise, and articulate in our messaging. We need to use language that is accessible and avoid jargon or technical terms that may alienate our audience. We also need to be confident and passionate in our delivery, conveying our conviction and inspiring others to believe in our vision.

Building trust is crucial for persuasion. People are more likely to be persuaded by someone they trust and respect. We can build trust by being honest, transparent, and consistent in our words and actions. We can also demonstrate our expertise and knowledge of the issues we are advocating for. By establishing ourselves as credible and trustworthy sources of information, we can increase our influence and persuade others to join our cause.

Persuasion is not a one-size-fits-all approach. Different people respond to different types of arguments and appeals. Some may be swayed by logic and reason, while others may be more responsive to emotional appeals or personal stories. By understanding the different styles of persuasion and adapting our approach accordingly, we can increase our effectiveness and reach a wider audience.

Active listening is a key component of persuasion. By listening attentively to others' perspectives, we can gain valuable insights into their concerns and motivations. We can also demonstrate respect for their views and build rapport. Active listening also allows us to identify common ground and tailor our message to address their specific needs and interests.

Negotiation is an important skill for persuasion. In politics, compromise is often necessary to achieve progress. By being willing to negotiate and find common ground, we can build coalitions and achieve our goals. Negotiation also requires us to be flexible and adaptable, willing to adjust our approach based on the situation and the needs of our partners.

Persistence is key to persuasion. It takes time and effort to change hearts and minds. We may encounter resistance, setbacks, and even outright opposition. But by staying focused on our goals, remaining persistent in our efforts, and never giving up on our vision, we can overcome obstacles and achieve lasting change.

The art of persuasion and influence is a lifelong journey. It requires continuous learning, practice, and refinement. By honing our skills, adapting to new situations, and building on our successes, we can become more effective advocates for our cause and inspire others to join us in creating a more just and equitable world.

ⵓⵓⵓ

"Fundraising is the fuel that propels your political aspirations. Cultivate relationships, inspire generosity, and diversify your sources. Remember, every contribution, no matter how small, is a brick in the foundation of your movement."

FOUR
NAVIGATING POLITICAL STRUCTURES

Navigating political structures is a critical skill for any woman who aspires to make a difference in the world. Political systems, whether local, national, or international, are complex webs of interconnected institutions, processes, and actors. Understanding these structures and learning how to navigate them effectively is essential for advancing our agendas, influencing decision-makers, and creating lasting change.

The first step in navigating political structures is to gain a comprehensive understanding of how they work. This involves learning about the different branches of government, the roles and responsibilities of elected officials, the legislative process, and the various mechanisms for public participation. It also requires understanding the informal networks and power dynamics that often shape political decision-making.

Building relationships is a crucial aspect of navigating political structures. We need to identify key stakeholders, build rapport with them, and establish ourselves as credible and trustworthy partners. This involves attending meetings, participating in events, and engaging in conversations with elected officials, community leaders, and other influential figures. By cultivating relationships with key players, we can gain access to information, influence decision-making, and build coalitions to support our goals.

Advocacy is a powerful tool for navigating political structures. By speaking out on issues we care about, mobilizing supporters, and engaging in public discourse, we can raise awareness, shape public opinion, and influence policy decisions. Effective advocacy involves developing compelling arguments, framing our message in a way that resonates with decision-makers, and building broad-based support for our cause.

Lobbying is another important strategy for navigating political structures. By meeting with elected officials and their staff, providing them with information and analysis, and advocating for our policy priorities, we can directly influence the legislative process. Effective lobbying involves building relationships with policymakers, understanding their priorities and constraints, and developing persuasive arguments that resonate with their values and interests.

Coalition building is a powerful way to amplify our voices and achieve our goals. By partnering with other organizations and individuals who share our values and interests, we can pool our resources, leverage our expertise, and mobilize our supporters to create a unified front. Effective coalition building involves identifying potential partners, building trust and rapport, and developing a shared vision and strategy for action.

Grassroots organizing is another important aspect of navigating political structures. By mobilizing our communities, engaging in direct action, and building a movement for change, we can create pressure on decision-makers and demand accountability. Effective grassroots organizing involves identifying and activating our base, developing effective communication and outreach strategies, and building a sustainable infrastructure for sustained action.

Using the media strategically is another essential tool for navigating political structures. By crafting compelling narratives, securing media coverage, and using social media to amplify our message, we can reach a wider audience, shape public opinion, and influence the political discourse. Effective media engagement involves developing relationships with journalists, understanding their needs and interests, and providing them with timely and accurate information.

Navigating political structures requires patience, persistence, and a willingness to adapt to changing circumstances. It's a long-term process that involves building relationships, developing strategies, and working collaboratively with others to achieve our goals. By understanding the political landscape, building coalitions, and engaging in effective advocacy, we can create lasting change and build a more just and equitable world.

As women, we bring unique perspectives and experiences to the political arena. By embracing our strengths, utilizing our skills, and working together, we can navigate political structures effectively and create a more inclusive and representative democracy.

ᐅᐅᐅ

"Your message is your weapon, a tool for shaping hearts and minds. Craft it with care, infuse it with passion, and deliver it with conviction. Let your words be a beacon of hope, a call to action, and a testament to your unwavering belief in a better future."

FIVE

Fundraising: Fueling Your Campaigns

Fundraising is the lifeblood of any political campaign. It is the fuel that powers the engine of change, enabling us to reach voters, spread our message, and mobilize support for our cause. For women in politics, fundraising can be a particular challenge, as we often face systemic barriers and biases that make it difficult to secure the resources we need to compete on a level playing field. However, with the right strategies and mindset, we can overcome these obstacles and build a sustainable fundraising program that fuels our campaigns and empowers us to make a difference.

At its core, fundraising is about building relationships and inspiring people to invest in our vision for a better future. It's about connecting with individuals and organizations who share our values and believe in our ability to make a difference. It's about articulating our message in a compelling way that resonates with donors and motivates them to contribute to our cause.

The first step in building a successful fundraising program is to develop a clear and comprehensive plan. This plan should outline our fundraising goals, target audience, strategies, and timeline. It should also include a budget that details our projected expenses and revenue sources. By having a well-defined plan in place, we can ensure that our fundraising efforts are focused, efficient, and effective.

Identifying potential donors is a critical aspect of fundraising. We need to research individuals and organizations who are likely to be interested in our cause and have the capacity to contribute financially. This involves building relationships with potential donors, attending events where they are likely to be present, and utilizing online tools and resources to identify potential prospects.

Building relationships with donors is essential for long-term fundraising success. We need to cultivate genuine connections with our supporters, thank them for their contributions, and keep them informed about our progress and impact. This can be done through regular communication, such as newsletters, emails, and social media updates. It can also involve hosting events and gatherings where donors can meet us and learn more about our work.

Diversifying our fundraising sources is important for building a sustainable program. We should not rely on a single source of funding, as this can make us vulnerable to fluctuations in the economy or changes in donor priorities. Instead, we should seek to build a diverse portfolio of funding sources, including individual donors, foundations, corporations, and political action committees.

Utilizing technology can be a powerful tool for fundraising. Online platforms and social media can be used to reach a wider audience, engage potential donors, and facilitate online donations. We can also use data analytics to track our fundraising progress, identify trends, and refine our strategies.

Ethical considerations are paramount in fundraising. We must always adhere to the highest standards of integrity and transparency. This means disclosing our fundraising practices, ensuring that all donations are used for their intended purpose, and avoiding any conflicts of interest. By maintaining ethical practices, we can build trust with our donors and ensure the long-term sustainability of our fundraising program.

Fundraising is not just about asking for money; it's about building a movement for change. By engaging with our supporters, sharing our vision, and inspiring them to invest in our cause, we can create a powerful network of advocates who are committed to our success. This network can provide not only financial support but also valuable resources, connections, and expertise.

As women in politics, we have a unique opportunity to inspire and empower other women to get involved in the political process. By sharing our stories, highlighting our accomplishments, and demonstrating the impact of our work, we can inspire other women to donate to our campaigns, volunteer their time, and even run for office themselves.

Fundraising is not always easy, but it is essential for achieving our goals and making a difference in the world. By developing a comprehensive plan, building relationships with donors, diversifying our funding sources, and utilizing technology effectively, we can build a sustainable fundraising program that fuels our campaigns and empowers us to create a more just and equitable society.

ppp

"Public speaking is the art of connection, a bridge between your vision and the hearts of your audience. Embrace your nervousness, channel your energy, and let your voice resonate with authenticity. Remember, your words have the power to inspire, motivate, and ignite change."

SIX
CRAFTING WINNING MESSAGES

Crafting winning messages is an art and a science, a delicate balance of substance and style, logic and emotion. In the realm of politics, where ideas clash and opinions abound, the ability to articulate a compelling message can be the difference between victory and defeat. For women in politics, who often face unique challenges and biases, mastering this skill is essential for cutting through the noise, resonating with voters, and building a movement for change.

At its core, a winning message is one that connects with people on a deep level, taps into their hopes and fears, and inspires them to action. It's a message that is clear, concise, and memorable, one that sticks in the minds of voters long after they've heard it. It's a message that speaks to their values, addresses their concerns, and offers a vision for a better future.

The first step in crafting a winning message is to identify our core values and priorities. What do we stand for? What are the issues that we care most about? What kind of change do we want to see in the world? By clarifying our values and priorities, we can begin to develop a message that is authentic, consistent, and resonant.

Once we have identified our core message, we need to tailor it to our audience. Who are we trying to reach? What are their concerns, interests, and values? By understanding our audience, we can frame our message in a way that speaks directly to their needs and aspirations. We can use language that is relatable and avoid jargon or technical terms that may alienate voters.

Storytelling is a powerful tool for crafting winning messages. By sharing personal anecdotes, case studies, and real-life examples, we can make our message more relatable and engaging. Stories have the power to evoke emotions, create connections, and inspire action. They can also help us break down complex issues into simple, understandable terms.

Repetition is another key element of crafting winning messages. By repeating our core message consistently across different platforms and channels, we can reinforce it in the minds of voters. We can use different variations of our message to keep it fresh and engaging, but we should always ensure that the core message remains clear and consistent.

A winning message should also be positive and hopeful. While it's important to acknowledge the challenges we face, we should focus on solutions and offer a vision for a better future. A positive message can inspire hope and optimism, while a negative message can breed cynicism and apathy.

Humor can also be a powerful tool in crafting winning messages. A well-timed joke or humorous anecdote can break the ice, put people at ease, and make our message more memorable. However, we should use humor judiciously and avoid anything that could be offensive or alienate voters.

A winning message should also be consistent with our actions. Our words should match our deeds. If we promise to fight for a particular issue, we need to follow through with concrete action. This will build credibility and trust with voters, and it will reinforce the power of our message.

In today's digital age, social media plays a crucial role in crafting and disseminating winning messages. We can use social media to reach a wider audience, engage with voters, and build a community of supporters. We can also use social media to test different messages and see what resonates with our target audience.

Crafting winning messages is an ongoing process. We need to constantly evaluate our message, refine it based on feedback, and adapt it to changing circumstances. By staying attuned to the needs and concerns of our constituents, we can ensure that our message remains relevant and impactful.

As women in politics, we have a unique perspective and a powerful voice. By crafting winning messages that resonate with voters, we can inspire action, build a movement for change, and create a more just and equitable world for all.

ppp

"The media can be a double-edged sword, a platform for amplification or distortion. Be strategic, build relationships, and control your narrative. Remember, your image is your brand, and your brand is your legacy."

SEVEN
MASTERING PUBLIC SPEAKING

Mastering public speaking is a transformative journey for any woman aspiring to lead, influence, or advocate. It's more than simply standing in front of an audience and delivering a speech. It's about connecting with people on a deep level, inspiring action, and leaving a lasting impact. For women in particular, who may face societal barriers and biases, developing strong public speaking skills is crucial for establishing credibility, amplifying their voices, and achieving their goals.

At its core, public speaking is about communication—conveying ideas, emotions, and information in a way that resonates with your audience. It's about building a rapport with your listeners, establishing trust, and inspiring them to share your vision. Effective public speaking involves a combination of preparation, technique, and mindset.

Preparation is key to delivering a successful speech. It starts with thorough research and understanding of your topic. Knowing your subject matter inside out allows you to speak with confidence and authority. It also enables you to anticipate and address potential questions or objections from your audience.

Crafting a well-structured speech is essential for keeping your audience engaged and focused. A clear introduction that captures attention, a well-organized body that presents your main points logically, and a strong conclusion that leaves a lasting impression are all crucial components of a successful speech.

Practice is essential for honing your delivery. Rehearsing your speech multiple times helps you become familiar with the material, smooth out any rough edges, and develop a natural flow. It also allows you to identify areas where you can improve your delivery, such as pacing, tone, and body language.

Overcoming nervousness is a common challenge for many public speakers, especially women who may face additional scrutiny and pressure. However, there are several techniques for managing anxiety, such as deep breathing exercises, visualization, and positive self-talk. Remember, even the most experienced speakers feel some level of nervousness before a presentation. The key is to channel that energy into a positive, engaging performance.

Connecting with your audience is essential for creating a meaningful impact. Eye contact, facial expressions, and gestures can all help you establish a connection with your listeners. Using inclusive language and avoiding jargon can make your message more accessible and relatable. Humor can also be a powerful tool for building rapport and keeping your audience engaged.

Vocal variety is another important aspect of public speaking. Varying your pitch, tone, and pace can help you emphasize key points, convey emotion, and keep your audience interested. A monotone voice can quickly bore listeners, while a dynamic delivery can captivate them and make your message more memorable.

Effective storytelling can be a powerful way to engage your audience and make your message more impactful. By sharing personal anecdotes, case studies, or real-life examples, you can illustrate your points, connect with your listeners on an emotional level, and make your message more memorable.

The use of visual aids, such as slides, charts, or images, can enhance your presentation and make complex information more accessible. However, it's important to use visual aids sparingly and ensure that they support your message rather than distract from it.

Active listening is a crucial skill for public speaking. Paying attention to your audience's reactions and adjusting your delivery accordingly can help you ensure that your message is resonating. It also demonstrates respect for your listeners and can help you build rapport.

Q&A sessions can be a valuable opportunity to engage with your audience, clarify your message, and address any concerns or objections. Preparing for potential questions and practicing your responses can help you feel more confident and prepared.

Mastering public speaking is a continuous journey of learning and growth. By embracing feedback, seeking out mentorship, and continuously practicing your skills, you can become a more confident and effective communicator. Remember, public speaking is not just about delivering a speech; it's about inspiring others, creating change, and leaving a lasting legacy.

For women in politics, public speaking is a powerful tool for breaking down barriers, challenging stereotypes, and amplifying their voices. By mastering this skill, women can become more effective leaders, advocates, and changemakers.

ᕕᕕᕕ

"Authenticity is your superpower, a beacon of truth in a world of artifice. Embrace your uniqueness, lead with your values, and inspire others with your genuineness. Remember, true leadership is not about fitting in; it's about standing out."

EIGHT

THE MEDIA: FRIEND OR FOE?

The media, a powerful force in shaping public opinion and influencing political discourse, can be both a friend and a foe to women in the political arena. It can be a platform for amplifying our voices, highlighting our achievements, and promoting our agendas. However, it can also perpetuate harmful stereotypes, undermine our credibility, and distort our message. Navigating this complex relationship requires a strategic approach, a keen understanding of the media landscape, and a willingness to engage with journalists on our own terms.

The media can be a powerful ally in our quest for political empowerment. It can shine a spotlight on issues that matter to women, such as gender equality, reproductive rights, and economic justice. It can showcase the accomplishments of women leaders, inspiring others to follow in their footsteps. It can also provide a platform for women to share their stories, perspectives, and experiences, challenging stereotypes and broadening the public discourse.

However, the media can also be a formidable foe. It can perpetuate harmful stereotypes about women, portraying us as emotional, irrational, or unqualified for leadership roles. It can focus on our appearance, personal lives, and family status, rather than our qualifications and achievements. It can also give disproportionate attention to negative stories or controversies, undermining our credibility and distracting from our message.

The rise of social media has further complicated the relationship between women in politics and the media. On the one hand, social media provides a powerful platform for women to connect with voters, share their message, and build a community of supporters. On the other hand, it can also be a breeding ground for misinformation, harassment, and abuse, disproportionately targeting women and minorities.

To navigate this complex landscape, women in politics need to develop a strategic approach to media engagement. This involves building relationships with journalists, understanding their needs and interests, and providing them with timely and accurate information. It also involves crafting compelling narratives that resonate with the public, utilizing social media effectively, and responding to negative coverage in a proactive and constructive manner.

Building relationships with journalists is crucial for securing positive media coverage. This involves identifying journalists who cover the issues we care about, reaching out to them with story ideas, and providing them with access to information and sources. By establishing ourselves as credible and reliable sources, we can increase our chances of being featured in news stories and opinion pieces.

Crafting compelling narratives is essential for capturing the media's attention and shaping public opinion. This involves identifying the key messages we want to convey, framing them in a way that resonates with the public, and using storytelling techniques to make our message more relatable and engaging. It also involves developing a clear and concise media strategy that outlines our goals, target audience, and tactics.

Utilizing social media effectively is another important aspect of media engagement. Social media platforms can be used to reach a wider audience, engage with voters, and build a community of supporters. However, it's important to use social media strategically, focusing on quality over quantity, and ensuring that our message is consistent across different platforms.

Responding to negative coverage is a delicate but important task. Ignoring negative stories or attacks can be detrimental, as it can allow misinformation to spread and damage our reputation. However, responding aggressively or defensively can also backfire. Instead, we should respond in a calm and measured manner, correcting any factual inaccuracies, highlighting our positive achievements, and focusing on our message.

The media can be a powerful tool for women in politics, but it's important to approach it with caution and strategy. By understanding the media landscape, building relationships with journalists, crafting compelling narratives, and utilizing social media effectively, we can harness the power of the media to amplify our voices, promote our agendas, and achieve our goals.

ᐅᐅᐅ

"Obstacles are stepping stones to success, challenges that test your resilience and fuel your determination. Embrace them, learn from them, and let them propel you forward. Remember, it is in overcoming adversity that we discover our true strength."

NINE

LEADING WITH AUTHENTICITY

Authenticity in leadership is more than just a buzzword. It is the cornerstone of building trust, inspiring others, and driving meaningful change. For women in politics, leading with authenticity can be a powerful differentiator, a way to cut through the noise and connect with voters on a deeper level. It is about being true to oneself, embracing one's values, and leading with integrity.

Authentic leadership begins with self-awareness. It requires a deep understanding of one's strengths, weaknesses, values, and motivations. It is about recognizing one's unique identity and embracing it as a source of strength. When we are self-aware, we are better equipped to lead with authenticity, make sound decisions, and build strong relationships.

Authentic leaders are transparent and honest. They communicate openly and honestly with their constituents, sharing their thoughts, feelings, and experiences. They are not afraid to admit their mistakes or ask for help. This transparency builds trust and fosters a culture of openness and collaboration.

Authentic leaders are driven by their values. They have a clear sense of purpose and are committed to making a positive impact on the world. Their values guide their decisions and actions, and they inspire others to share their vision. When we lead with our values, we create a sense of meaning and purpose that resonates with others.

Authentic leaders are compassionate and empathetic. They understand the needs and concerns of their constituents and are committed to serving their interests. They listen to different perspectives, seek to understand different viewpoints, and build bridges across divides. When we lead with compassion, we create a more inclusive and equitable society.

Authenticity in leadership is not about being perfect. It's about being human. It's about acknowledging our flaws and imperfections while striving to be our best selves. When we show our vulnerability, we create a space for others to do the same. This can lead to deeper connections, greater trust, and more effective collaboration.

Authenticity in leadership is also about empowering others. It's about creating a culture where everyone feels valued, respected, and heard. It's about giving people the tools and resources they need to succeed and encouraging them to reach their full potential. When we empower others, we create a more engaged and productive workforce.

Leading with authenticity can be challenging, especially in the political arena, where image and perception often take precedence over substance. However, the benefits of authenticity far outweigh the challenges. When we lead with authenticity, we build trust, inspire others, and create a more positive and productive work environment.

Authenticity is not a static quality; it is a dynamic process. It requires continuous self-reflection, growth, and development. As we evolve as individuals and leaders, our understanding of authenticity may also change. It's important to remain open to new experiences, feedback, and perspectives, and to constantly challenge ourselves to grow and learn.

In the ever-changing landscape of politics, authenticity is a timeless virtue. It is a quality that transcends party lines, ideologies, and demographics. It is a quality that resonates with people across the political spectrum and inspires them to believe in a better future.

For women in politics, leading with authenticity can be a game-changer. It can help us break down barriers, challenge stereotypes, and build a more inclusive and representative democracy. By being true to ourselves, embracing our values, and leading with integrity, we can inspire others to do the same.

ᐅᐅᐅ

"Mentorship is the gift that keeps on giving, a legacy of empowerment passed down through generations. Share your knowledge, guide the next generation, and watch your impact ripple through time. Remember, the seeds you plant today will blossom into the leaders of tomorrow."

TEN

OVERCOMING OBSTACLES AND BIAS

The path to political empowerment for women is fraught with obstacles and biases, deeply ingrained in societal structures and cultural norms. These challenges can manifest in various forms, from outright discrimination to subtle microaggressions, from institutional barriers to internalized self-doubt. However, these obstacles are not insurmountable. By acknowledging their existence, understanding their roots, and developing strategies to overcome them, women can not only navigate the political landscape but also reshape it to be more inclusive and equitable.

One of the most pervasive obstacles faced by women in politics is the persistence of gender stereotypes. Women are often judged based on their appearance, demeanor, and perceived "feminine" qualities, rather than their qualifications and experience. They may be seen as too emotional, too soft, or not tough enough to handle the rigors of political office. These stereotypes can undermine women's credibility, limit their opportunities, and discourage them from pursuing political careers.

Another significant obstacle is the lack of representation of women in politics. Despite making up half of the world's population, women remain underrepresented in political institutions at all levels. This lack of representation can create a vicious cycle, as the absence of women role models can discourage young girls and women from aspiring to political leadership. It also means that women's voices and perspectives are often excluded from the decision-making process, leading to policies that may not adequately address their needs and concerns.

Institutional barriers also pose a significant challenge for women in politics. These barriers can take many forms, from discriminatory laws and regulations to informal practices and norms that favor men. For example, women may face difficulty accessing financial resources for their campaigns, securing endorsements from party leaders, or navigating the often male-dominated culture of political institutions.

Internalized biases can also be a major obstacle for women in politics. Many women have been socialized to believe that they are not as capable or qualified as men, or that politics is not a suitable field for them. These internalized biases can lead to self-doubt, hesitation, and a reluctance to put oneself forward for leadership roles.

Overcoming these obstacles and biases requires a multi-pronged approach. First and foremost, it requires raising awareness about the issue. By educating the public about the challenges faced by women in politics, we can start to change attitudes and perceptions. We can also work to dismantle stereotypes by highlighting the accomplishments of women leaders and showcasing the diversity of women's experiences and perspectives.

Building a strong support network is also crucial for women in politics. Mentorship programs, women's caucuses, and other networking opportunities can provide valuable resources, guidance, and encouragement. By connecting with other women who have faced similar challenges, we can learn from their experiences, share strategies for success, and build a community of support.

Developing the skills and knowledge necessary for political leadership is also essential. This includes learning about the political process, public policy, communication, and negotiation. Many organizations and programs offer training and resources specifically for women who are interested in pursuing political careers.

Advocating for systemic change is another important step in overcoming obstacles and biases. This can involve working to change discriminatory laws and regulations, promoting gender quotas in political institutions, and challenging informal practices and norms that perpetuate gender inequality.

Perhaps most importantly, overcoming obstacles and biases requires a shift in mindset. Women need to believe in their own abilities, challenge their internalized biases, and refuse to let societal expectations hold them back. It also requires a willingness to speak out against injustice, challenge the status quo, and demand a seat at the table.

The journey to political empowerment is not an easy one, but it is a necessary one. By overcoming obstacles and biases, women can not only achieve their own political aspirations but also create a more inclusive and equitable society .

ᐅᐅᐅ

"Collaboration is the cornerstone of progress, a symphony of diverse voices united in a common cause. Seek out allies, build bridges, and amplify your impact through collective action. Remember, together, we can achieve what we could never accomplish alone."

ELEVEN

MENTORING THE NEXT GENERATION

Mentoring the next generation of women leaders is not just a responsibility; it's a privilege, a legacy, and a catalyst for lasting change. It's a torch passed from one generation to the next, illuminating the path to political empowerment and inspiring young women to reach their full potential. For women who have broken barriers, shattered glass ceilings, and achieved success in their own right, mentoring offers a unique opportunity to share their knowledge, experience, and wisdom, paving the way for a more inclusive and equitable political landscape.

Mentorship is a reciprocal relationship, a two-way street where both mentor and mentee benefit from the exchange. For mentors, it's a chance to give back, to share their hard-earned lessons, and to inspire the next generation of leaders. It's a way to ensure that their legacy lives on, that their accomplishments are not just personal milestones but stepping stones for others to follow.

For mentees, mentorship provides invaluable guidance, support, and encouragement. It's a safe space to ask questions, seek advice, and learn from the experiences of those who have gone before. It's a source of inspiration and motivation, a reminder that their dreams are achievable and that they have the potential to make a difference in the world.

Mentorship can take many forms, from formal programs to informal relationships. It can be a one-on-one connection between a seasoned leader and a budding activist, or a group mentoring program that brings together women from different backgrounds and experiences. Regardless of the format, effective mentorship is characterized by trust, respect, and a shared commitment to empowering women.

Mentoring is not just about imparting knowledge and skills; it's about fostering a sense of belonging and empowerment. It's about creating a community where women can lift each other up, celebrate their achievements, and learn from their setbacks. It's about providing a platform for women to share their stories, perspectives, and aspirations, and to develop the confidence and resilience needed to navigate the challenges of political life.

One of the most important aspects of mentoring is providing guidance and advice. Mentors can share their own experiences, offer insights into the political process, and help mentees develop strategies for overcoming obstacles and achieving their goals. They can also provide feedback on mentees' work, offer constructive criticism, and help them refine their skills and knowledge.

Mentorship can also provide access to networks and opportunities that may otherwise be difficult to reach. Mentors can introduce mentees to influential people, open doors to internships and jobs, and provide access to resources and information. This can be invaluable for young women who are just starting out in their political careers and may not have established connections or networks.

Mentorship can also be a source of emotional support and

encouragement. The political arena can be a challenging and isolating environment, especially for women. Mentors can offer a listening ear, provide a safe space to vent frustrations, and offer words of encouragement and support. This can be crucial for helping mentees maintain their resilience and motivation in the face of adversity.

Mentoring is not a one-way street. Mentees also have a responsibility to be active participants in the relationship. They should be eager to learn, open to feedback, and willing to take initiative. They should also be respectful of their mentors' time and expertise, and grateful for their guidance and support.

Mentorship is a lifelong journey. It doesn't end when the formal mentorship program or relationship is over. The lessons learned, the connections made, and the support received can continue to shape and inspire women throughout their political careers. In turn, as mentees grow and develop, they can become mentors themselves, passing on the torch to the next generation.

The power of mentorship to empower women in politics cannot be overstated. By sharing our knowledge, experience, and wisdom, we can create a ripple effect that extends far beyond our individual reach. We can inspire a new generation of women leaders who are bold, confident, and committed to creating a more just and equitable world.

ppp

"From activism to policy, your journey is a testament to the power of perseverance and strategic action. Learn the language of power, build coalitions, and translate your passion into tangible change. Remember, your voice matters, and your actions can shape the future."

TWELVE
THE POWER OF COLLABORATION

Collaboration is the cornerstone of progress, a symphony of diverse voices and perspectives harmonizing to create lasting change. In the political arena, where power dynamics often favor the few, collaboration empowers the many. It's a force multiplier, a means of amplifying individual voices and leveraging collective strength to achieve shared goals. For women in politics, who often face systemic barriers and biases, collaboration is not just a strategy; it's a necessity.

The power of collaboration lies in its ability to transcend differences and unite people around a common cause. It's about recognizing that we are stronger together than we are alone. By joining forces with other women, we can pool our resources, leverage our expertise, and mobilize our supporters to achieve goals that would be impossible to reach individually.

Collaboration is not about conformity or compromise; it's about embracing diversity and leveraging the unique strengths of each individual. It's about creating a space where everyone feels valued, respected, and heard. It's about building trust and fostering a culture of mutual support and collaboration. When we collaborate with others, we expand our horizons, challenge our assumptions, and learn from different perspectives.

In the political sphere, collaboration can take many forms. It can involve working with other women candidates or elected officials to advance a shared agenda. It can involve partnering with grassroots organizations and community groups to mobilize support for a particular issue. It can also involve building coalitions with diverse stakeholders, such as businesses, labor unions, and faith-based organizations, to create a broad-based movement for change.

The benefits of collaboration are numerous. By working together, we can achieve greater impact, reach a wider audience, and build a more sustainable movement for change. Collaboration can also help us overcome obstacles and challenges that we might face individually. By sharing resources, expertise, and support, we can navigate complex issues and find innovative solutions to seemingly intractable problems.

Collaboration also fosters a sense of community and belonging. When we work together towards a common goal, we forge strong bonds with others who share our passion and commitment. This sense of community can be a powerful source of motivation and support, especially in the face of adversity.

Effective collaboration requires a willingness to listen, learn, and compromise. It's about finding common ground, building consensus, and working towards a shared vision. It also requires a commitment to open communication, transparency, and accountability. When we collaborate with others, we need to be willing to share credit, acknowledge our mistakes, and learn from our experiences.

Building and maintaining successful collaborations can be challenging. It requires time, effort, and a willingness to invest in relationships. It also requires a commitment to overcoming differences, resolving conflicts, and finding ways to work together effectively. However, the rewards of collaboration far outweigh the challenges.

For women in politics, collaboration is not just a good idea; it's a strategic imperative. By working together, we can break down barriers, overcome biases, and create a more inclusive and equitable political system. We can amplify our voices, leverage our collective strength, and achieve lasting change.

Collaboration is not a sign of weakness; it's a sign of strength. It's a recognition that we are all part of something bigger than ourselves. It's a commitment to working together to build a better future for all.

ppp

"The political landscape is a chessboard, a game of strategy and influence. Master the art of negotiation, build alliances, and always be prepared to compromise. Remember, the goal is not to win every battle, but to win the war for a better world."

THIRTEEN

FROM ACTIVISM TO POLICY

The journey from activism to policy is a transformative one, a testament to the power of collective action and the unwavering belief that change is possible. It's a path often fraught with challenges, requiring perseverance, strategic thinking, and a deep understanding of the political landscape. But for those who dare to tread it, the rewards are immeasurable: the opportunity to shape laws, influence institutions, and create a more just and equitable society.

Activism, at its core, is about raising awareness, mobilizing support, and demanding change. It's about giving voice to the voiceless, challenging the status quo, and advocating for a better future. Activists are the disruptors, the agitators, the ones who dare to dream of a different world and work tirelessly to make it a reality.

But activism alone is not enough. To create lasting change, we need to translate our passion and energy into concrete policy solutions. We need to move from the streets to the halls of power, from protest signs to legislative bills. This transition requires a shift in strategy, a deeper understanding of the political process, and a willingness to engage with those in power.

The first step in moving from activism to policy is to develop a clear and comprehensive policy agenda. This involves identifying the root causes of the problems we are trying to address, researching evidence-based solutions, and crafting policy proposals that are both ambitious and achievable. It also requires building a coalition of support, bringing together diverse stakeholders who share our vision for change.

Once we have a policy agenda in place, we need to engage with policymakers and decision-makers. This can involve meeting with elected officials, testifying before legislative committees, and submitting written comments on proposed legislation. It also requires building relationships with key influencers, such as community leaders, academics, and industry experts, who can lend their voices and expertise to our cause.

Advocacy is a crucial tool for influencing policy. By raising awareness about our issue, educating the public, and mobilizing support, we can create pressure on policymakers to act. Effective advocacy involves developing compelling messages, utilizing a variety of communication channels, and building a broad-based coalition of supporters.

Lobbying is another important strategy for influencing policy. This involves direct communication with policymakers and their staff, providing them with information and analysis, and advocating for specific policy changes. Effective lobbying requires building relationships with policymakers, understanding their priorities and constraints, and developing persuasive arguments that resonate with their values and interests.

Grassroots organizing is also essential for moving from activism to policy. By mobilizing our communities, engaging in direct action, and building a movement for change, we can create pressure on policymakers to act. Effective grassroots organizing involves identifying and activating our base, developing effective communication and outreach strategies, and building a sustainable infrastructure for sustained action.

The transition from activism to policy is not always a smooth one. We may encounter resistance, setbacks, and even outright opposition. But by staying focused on our goals, remaining persistent in our efforts, and building strong coalitions, we can overcome these challenges and achieve lasting change.

The journey from activism to policy is not just about changing laws and regulations; it's about transforming our society and creating a more just and equitable world. It's about empowering individuals and communities to take control of their own lives and shape their own destinies. It's about building a future where everyone has the opportunity to thrive, regardless of their background or circumstances.

ppp

"Balancing personal and political life is a delicate dance, a constant negotiation between your public and private selves. Set boundaries, prioritize self-care, and never lose sight of what truly matters. Remember, your well-being is the foundation of your leadership."

FOURTEEN

Negotiating the Political Landscape

The political landscape is a dynamic and often challenging arena, a space where diverse interests collide, alliances shift, and power dynamics constantly evolve. For women who aspire to lead and influence in this arena, mastering the art of negotiation is paramount. It's a skill that empowers us to bridge divides, find common ground, and forge coalitions that can drive meaningful change.

Negotiation is not just about winning or losing; it's about finding solutions that meet the needs and interests of all parties involved. It's about building trust, establishing rapport, and creating win-win outcomes that advance our shared goals. In the political realm, where compromise is often necessary to achieve progress, negotiation skills are indispensable.

Effective negotiation begins with a clear understanding of our own goals and priorities. What are we trying to achieve? What are our non-negotiables? What are we willing to compromise on? By having a clear sense of our own interests, we can approach negotiations with confidence and clarity.

It's equally important to understand the needs and interests of the other parties involved. What are their motivations? What are their concerns? What are they willing to concede? By understanding their perspective, we can identify potential areas of agreement and develop creative solutions that address everyone's needs.

Preparation is key to successful negotiation. Before entering into any negotiation, we need to gather information, research the issue at hand, and develop a clear strategy. We need to anticipate potential obstacles, identify areas of leverage, and prepare for different scenarios. By being well-prepared, we can approach negotiations with confidence and flexibility.

Active listening is a crucial component of negotiation. By listening attentively to the other side, we can gain valuable insights into their perspective, identify their underlying concerns, and build rapport. Active listening also allows us to identify potential areas of agreement and tailor our approach accordingly.

Effective communication is essential for negotiation. We need to be clear, concise, and articulate in expressing our own needs and interests, as well as understanding those of others. We also need to be respectful, empathetic, and open to different perspectives. By communicating effectively, we can build trust, foster collaboration, and increase the chances of reaching a mutually beneficial agreement.

Building relationships is a crucial aspect of negotiation. By establishing rapport and trust with the other parties involved, we can create a more positive and productive negotiating environment. This involves being genuine, respectful, and empathetic. It also involves finding common ground, highlighting shared values, and building a sense of shared purpose.

Flexibility and adaptability are essential for navigating the ever-changing political landscape. We need to be willing to adjust our approach, consider new information, and compromise when necessary. Rigidity and intransigence can derail negotiations and lead to impasse. By being flexible and adaptable, we can increase our chances of reaching a successful outcome.

Negotiation is not a one-time event; it's an ongoing process. Even after an agreement has been reached, we need to continue to build relationships, monitor progress, and address any issues that may arise. By maintaining open communication and a collaborative spirit, we can ensure that the agreement is implemented effectively and that our shared goals are achieved.

Negotiation is a powerful tool for women in politics. It allows us to bridge divides, build coalitions, and achieve our goals. By mastering the art of negotiation, we can become more effective leaders, advocates, and changemakers.

ᐯᐯᐯ

"Campaign strategies are the roadmaps to victory, the blueprints for transforming your vision into reality. Be strategic, data-driven, and always put the needs of your constituents first. Remember, a successful campaign is not just about winning an election; it's about building a movement."

FIFTEEN

BALANCING PERSONAL AND POLITICAL LIFE

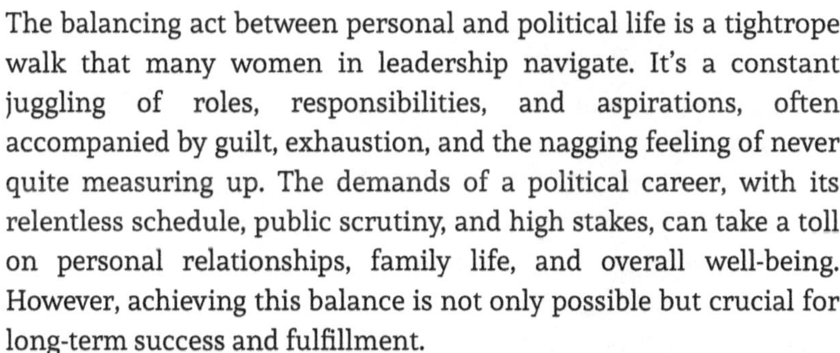

The balancing act between personal and political life is a tightrope walk that many women in leadership navigate. It's a constant juggling of roles, responsibilities, and aspirations, often accompanied by guilt, exhaustion, and the nagging feeling of never quite measuring up. The demands of a political career, with its relentless schedule, public scrutiny, and high stakes, can take a toll on personal relationships, family life, and overall well-being. However, achieving this balance is not only possible but crucial for long-term success and fulfillment.

The first step in achieving balance is recognizing that it's an ongoing process, not a destination. There will be times when one aspect of life takes precedence over the other. The key is to be intentional about how we allocate our time and energy, and to make choices that align with our values and priorities.

Setting clear boundaries between personal and political life is essential. This can involve creating dedicated time for family and friends, establishing routines and rituals that promote self-care, and learning to say no to requests that don't align with our priorities. It's also important to communicate our boundaries to others, so they understand our needs and respect our time.

Building a strong support system is crucial for maintaining balance. This can include family, friends, mentors, colleagues, and even professional coaches or therapists. Having people who we can confide in, seek advice from, and lean on for emotional support can make all the difference in navigating the challenges of a demanding career.

Prioritizing self-care is not a luxury; it's a necessity. This can involve taking time for exercise, relaxation, hobbies, and other activities that nourish our bodies and minds. It can also involve setting aside time for reflection, mindfulness, and spiritual practice. When we take care of ourselves, we are better equipped to handle the demands of our political careers and personal lives.

Delegation is another important tool for achieving balance. We cannot do everything ourselves, and trying to do so will only lead to burnout. By delegating tasks to trusted colleagues, family members, or even paid professionals, we can free up our time and energy to focus on the things that matter most.

Learning to say no is a crucial skill for maintaining balance. We are constantly bombarded with requests for our time and attention, and it's impossible to say yes to everything. By learning to say no to requests that don't align with our priorities, we can protect our time and energy for the things that matter most.

Flexibility is key to navigating the unpredictable nature of both personal and political life. Unexpected events, crises, and opportunities can arise at any time, and we need to be able to adapt and adjust our plans accordingly. By cultivating a flexible mindset, we can embrace change and find creative solutions to challenges.

Communication is essential for maintaining healthy relationships with our loved ones. By openly communicating our needs, concerns, and challenges, we can build trust, strengthen our bonds, and ensure that our loved ones feel supported and understood.

Balancing personal and political life is not always easy, but it is possible. By setting clear boundaries, building a strong support system, prioritizing self-care, delegating tasks, learning to say no, being flexible, and communicating openly, we can create a fulfilling and sustainable life that honors both our personal and professional aspirations.

Remember, we are not alone in this journey. Many women have successfully navigated the challenges of balancing personal and political life. By learning from their experiences, seeking out mentorship and support, and prioritizing our own well-being, we too can achieve balance and thrive in both spheres of our lives.

ᐅᐅᐅ

"Technology is a powerful tool, a force multiplier for political change. Embrace it, utilize it strategically, and harness its potential to connect, mobilize, and inspire. Remember, the future of politics is digital, and you are at the forefront of this revolution."

SIXTEEN

CAMPAIGN STRATEGIES THAT WORK

In the intricate dance of politics, campaign strategies are the carefully choreographed steps that lead to victory. They are the blueprints that transform aspirations into actions, visions into votes. For women aspiring to political office, crafting effective campaign strategies is not just about winning an election; it's about dismantling barriers, challenging norms, and redefining leadership. It's about creating a movement that resonates with voters, empowers communities, and paves the way for a more inclusive and equitable society.

A successful campaign strategy is not a one-size-fits-all formula. It's a dynamic and adaptable plan that evolves with the changing political landscape. It's a combination of art and science, blending creativity with data-driven insights, intuition with evidence-based decision-making. It's about understanding the unique challenges and opportunities facing women candidates and crafting a strategy that leverages their strengths and addresses their weaknesses.

At the heart of any successful campaign strategy is a compelling message. This message should be clear, concise, and resonate with voters' concerns and aspirations. It should articulate a vision for the future that inspires hope and optimism, while also addressing the pressing issues facing the community. A strong message should also be consistent across all campaign platforms and channels, from social media to stump speeches to campaign literature.

Building a strong team is another crucial element of a winning campaign strategy. A campaign team should be diverse, reflecting the demographics of the community it seeks to represent. It should also be composed of individuals with a wide range of skills and expertise, from fundraising and communications to field organizing and data analysis. A strong team can provide the support, guidance, and infrastructure needed to run a successful campaign.

Fundraising is the lifeblood of any political campaign. Without adequate financial resources, it's impossible to reach voters, spread our message, and mobilize support. Successful campaigns develop a comprehensive fundraising plan that targets a variety of donors, from small-dollar individual contributors to large institutional donors. They also leverage online platforms and social media to reach a wider audience and streamline the donation process.

Effective communication is essential for any campaign. This involves developing a comprehensive communications plan that outlines the key messages, target audience, and communication channels. It also involves crafting compelling content, utilizing social media effectively, and engaging with the media in a strategic and proactive manner. A strong communications strategy can help build name recognition, generate positive media coverage, and connect with voters on a personal level.

Community engagement is a cornerstone of successful campaigns.

By reaching out to voters directly, listening to their concerns, and offering solutions to their problems, we can build trust, earn their support, and mobilize them to action. Effective community engagement involves attending community events, hosting town halls, canvassing neighborhoods, and utilizing social media to connect with voters online.

Data-driven decision-making is another critical component of modern campaign strategies. By collecting and analyzing data on voter demographics, preferences, and behaviors, we can tailor our message, target our outreach, and optimize our resources. Data can also help us identify potential supporters, track the effectiveness of our campaign tactics, and make informed decisions about where to focus our efforts.

Technology plays an increasingly important role in political campaigns. From social media platforms to voter databases to online fundraising tools, technology can help us reach a wider audience, engage with voters more effectively, and streamline our operations. Successful campaigns embrace technology and utilize it to their advantage.

A winning campaign strategy is not just about winning an election; it's about building a movement for change. By focusing on issues that matter to voters, engaging with them directly, and offering a vision for a better future, we can inspire hope, mobilize support, and create lasting change in our communities and beyond.

ppp

"Your voice is your power, a beacon in the political landscape. Don't underestimate its impact; every whisper has the potential to ignite a movement. Speak your truth, for it is in your authenticity that your leadership truly shines."

SEVENTEEN

THE ROLE OF TECHNOLOGY IN POLITICS

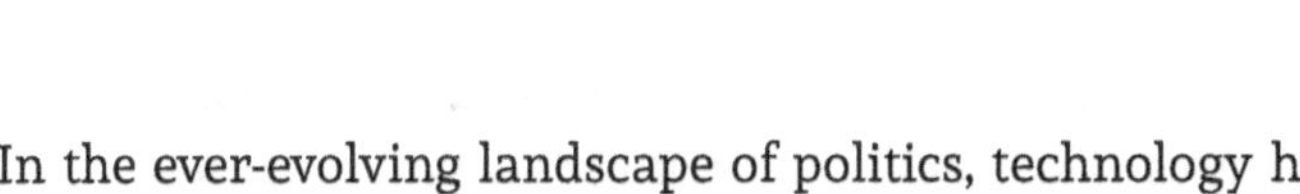

In the ever-evolving landscape of politics, technology has emerged as a formidable force, reshaping the way campaigns are run, constituents are engaged, and policies are formed. From the early days of radio broadcasts to the rise of social media and big data, technology has revolutionized the political arena, offering both opportunities and challenges for those who seek to lead and influence.

In the 20th century, the advent of radio and television transformed political communication. Leaders could now directly address the nation, bypassing traditional gatekeepers like newspapers and political parties. This democratization of information empowered voters with unprecedented access to political discourse, enabling them to make more informed decisions.

The rise of the internet in the late 20th century further accelerated this trend. Websites, email, and online forums provided new platforms for political expression, organizing, and activism.

Political campaigns began to leverage these tools to reach voters, mobilize supporters, and raise funds. The internet also facilitated the emergence of new political movements and organizations, challenging traditional power structures and giving voice to marginalized groups.

The 21st century has seen the explosion of social media, transforming the way we communicate, connect, and consume information. Social media platforms like Facebook, Twitter, and Instagram have become powerful tools for political campaigns, enabling them to reach vast audiences, engage with voters in real-time, and mobilize support for their cause. Social media has also democratized political discourse, giving ordinary citizens a platform to express their views, challenge established narratives, and hold leaders accountable.

However, the rise of social media has also brought new challenges to the political arena. The proliferation of fake news, misinformation, and echo chambers has raised concerns about the integrity of political discourse and the ability of voters to make informed decisions. Social media platforms have also been criticized for their role in amplifying extremist views, fostering polarization, and facilitating foreign interference in elections.

Big data and analytics have also transformed the way political campaigns are run. By collecting and analyzing vast amounts of data on voter demographics, preferences, and behaviors, campaigns can tailor their messages, target their outreach, and optimize their resources. This data-driven approach can be highly effective in identifying and mobilizing supporters, but it also raises concerns about privacy, surveillance, and the potential for manipulation.

Artificial intelligence (AI) is another emerging technology with significant implications for politics. AI-powered tools can be used to automate tasks, analyze data, and even generate content. While AI has the potential to streamline campaign operations and improve efficiency, it also raises ethical concerns about the use of algorithms in decision-making, the potential for bias and discrimination, and the impact on employment.

The rise of technology has also transformed the way governments operate and deliver services. E-government initiatives have made it easier for citizens to access information, interact with government agencies, and participate in the political process. Technology has also enabled governments to collect and analyze data on a massive scale, improving their ability to understand and respond to the needs of their citizens.

However, the increasing reliance on technology in government also raises concerns about cybersecurity, privacy, and the digital divide. As more and more government services move online, it's important to ensure that everyone has access to the technology and skills needed to participate in the digital age.

In conclusion, technology has played a pivotal role in shaping the modern political landscape. It has empowered voters, democratized political discourse, and transformed the way campaigns are run and governments operate. However, it has also brought new challenges, such as the spread of misinformation, the rise of echo chambers, and the potential for manipulation and surveillance. As we move forward, it's important to embrace the opportunities that technology offers while also addressing the challenges it presents. By doing so, we can harness the power of technology to build a more informed, engaged, and equitable society.

ppp

"Networks are the threads that weave a tapestry of change. Seek out those who share your vision, lift each other up, and together, create a force that cannot be ignored. Remember, united we stand, divided we fall."

EIGHTEEN

GRASSROOTS ORGANIZING: BUILDING MOMENTUM

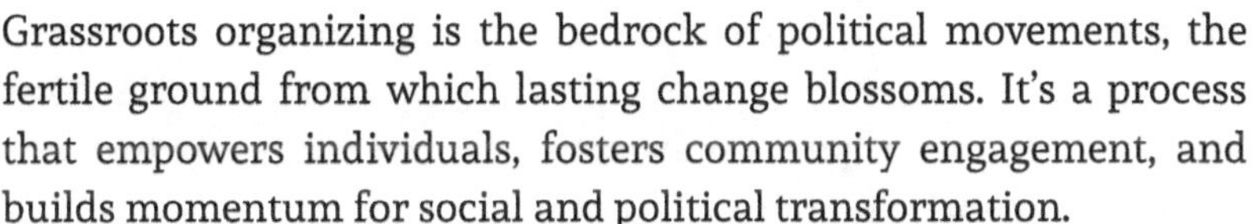

Grassroots organizing is the bedrock of political movements, the fertile ground from which lasting change blossoms. It's a process that empowers individuals, fosters community engagement, and builds momentum for social and political transformation.

At its heart, grassroots organizing is about mobilizing ordinary people to take collective action on issues that affect their lives. It's about creating a sense of shared purpose, building a network of relationships, and leveraging the power of collective action to challenge the status quo and advocate for a better future.

The essence of grassroots organizing lies in its bottom-up approach. It starts with identifying and connecting with individuals who are directly affected by a particular issue or concern.

These individuals, often overlooked or marginalized by traditional power structures, are the heart and soul of the movement. They bring their lived experiences, their passion, and their unique perspectives to the table, enriching the movement and ensuring that it remains grounded in the realities of the community.

Building relationships is a cornerstone of grassroots organizing. It's about fostering trust, respect, and solidarity among members of the community. It's about creating a space where people feel safe to share their stories, express their concerns, and work together towards a common goal.

These relationships are the foundation upon which a movement is built, providing the support, encouragement, and resilience needed to sustain momentum over the long term.

Leadership development is another crucial aspect of grassroots organizing. It's about identifying and nurturing leaders from within the community, empowering them to take ownership of the movement and drive its agenda. Effective leaders inspire others, build consensus, and create a vision for change that resonates with the broader community. They are the bridge between the grassroots and the corridors of power, advocating for the needs and interests of their constituents.

Education and awareness-raising are essential for building momentum. It's about informing the community about the issues at stake, providing them with the tools and resources they need to understand the problem, and empowering them to take action.

This can involve hosting workshops, distributing educational materials, and engaging in public awareness campaigns. By educating and empowering individuals, we can create a more informed and engaged citizenry that is ready to demand change.

Direct action is a powerful tool for grassroots organizing. It's about taking to the streets, engaging in protests, boycotts, and other forms of nonviolent resistance to draw attention to our cause and pressure decision-makers to act. Direct action can be a catalyst for change, mobilizing public support, and forcing those in power to take notice.

Building coalitions is another key strategy for grassroots organizing. By partnering with other organizations and individuals who share our goals, we can amplify our impact and create a broader movement for change. Coalitions bring together diverse perspectives, resources, and expertise, enabling us to tackle complex issues and achieve systemic change.

Utilizing technology is essential for modern grassroots organizing. Social media platforms, online forums, and other digital tools can be used to connect with supporters, share information, mobilize action, and build a community of like-minded individuals. Technology can also be used to collect and analyze data, track progress, and measure impact.

Grassroots organizing is not a quick fix; it's a long-term investment in building a more just and equitable society. It requires patience, perseverance, and a willingness to adapt to changing circumstances. It also requires a commitment to building relationships, empowering individuals, and creating a shared vision for change.

The momentum generated by grassroots organizing can be a powerful force for good. It can lead to the passage of new laws, the election of progressive candidates, and the transformation of social norms and values. It can also empower individuals and communities to take control of their own lives and shape their own destinies.

For women in politics, grassroots organizing is a particularly important tool. It allows us to bypass traditional power structures, build our own networks, and create our own path to leadership.

By harnessing the power of grassroots organizing, we can challenge the status quo, dismantle barriers, and create a more inclusive and equitable political landscape.

ᐅᐅᐅ

"Grassroots organizing is the heart and soul of political movements, the power of the people rising up to demand change. Connect with your community, build relationships, and unleash the collective power of your voices. Remember, change starts from the ground up."

NINETEEN

GOVERNING EFFECTIVELY: MAKING A DIFFERENCE

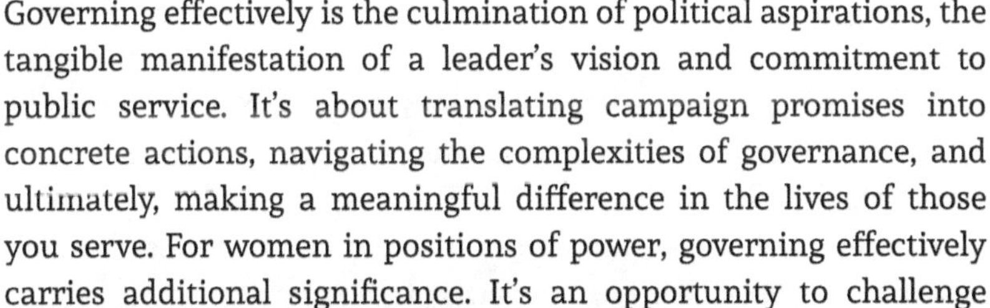

Governing effectively is the culmination of political aspirations, the tangible manifestation of a leader's vision and commitment to public service. It's about translating campaign promises into concrete actions, navigating the complexities of governance, and ultimately, making a meaningful difference in the lives of those you serve. For women in positions of power, governing effectively carries additional significance. It's an opportunity to challenge traditional norms, shatter glass ceilings, and demonstrate that women can lead with strength, compassion, and vision.

Effective governance is not simply about managing the day-to-day operations of government. It's about setting a strategic direction, making tough decisions, and balancing competing interests. It's about building consensus, inspiring collaboration, and fostering a culture of transparency and accountability. It's about creating policies that promote equity, justice, and opportunity for all.

At the heart of effective governance is a deep understanding of the needs and aspirations of the people you serve. This requires active listening, empathy, and a willingness to engage with diverse perspectives. It means seeking out input from community members, stakeholders, and experts, and incorporating their feedback into the decision-making process. Effective leaders understand that governance is not a top-down exercise; it's a collaborative effort that requires the participation and engagement of all members of society.

Effective governance also requires a clear vision for the future. This vision should be grounded in the values and priorities of the community, while also being ambitious and forward-thinking. It should articulate a clear direction for the government, outlining the goals to be achieved and the strategies to be employed. A compelling vision can inspire and motivate others, creating a sense of shared purpose and collective responsibility.

Transparency and accountability are essential for effective governance. Leaders must be open and honest about their decisions, their motivations, and the challenges they face. They must be willing to explain their reasoning, answer tough questions, and be held accountable for their actions. Transparency builds trust with the public, while accountability ensures that leaders remain responsive to the needs and concerns of their constituents.

Collaboration is another key element of effective governance. No leader can solve complex problems alone. Effective leaders recognize the importance of building coalitions, working across party lines, and engaging with diverse stakeholders to find common ground and develop solutions that work for everyone. Collaboration also fosters a sense of shared ownership and responsibility, which can lead to more effective and sustainable outcomes.

Effective governance requires a commitment to continuous learning and improvement. Leaders must be willing to adapt their strategies, embrace new ideas, and learn from their mistakes. They must also be open to feedback, both positive and negative, and use it to refine their approach and improve their performance.

Inclusivity is a fundamental principle of effective governance. Leaders must ensure that all voices are heard and that everyone has an equal opportunity to participate in the political process. This means creating spaces for dialogue and engagement, actively seeking out diverse perspectives, and ensuring that policies and programs are designed to meet the needs of all members of the community.

Effective governance also requires a focus on results. Leaders must set clear goals, track progress, and measure the impact of their policies and programs. They must be willing to adjust their course when necessary and be held accountable for their results. By focusing on results, leaders can ensure that their efforts are making a real difference in the lives of the people they serve.

For women in leadership, effective governance is an opportunity to demonstrate that women can lead with strength, compassion, and vision. It's a chance to challenge stereotypes, break down barriers, and inspire a new generation of women leaders. By leading with authenticity, embracing collaboration, and focusing on results, women leaders can create a more inclusive, equitable, and prosperous society for all.

ᐅᐅᐅ

"Governing effectively is the ultimate test of
leadership, the opportunity to translate your vision
into reality. Be transparent, accountable, and
collaborative. Focus on results, not just rhetoric,
and always put the needs of your people first.
Remember, your legacy is defined by the impact you
make on the world."

TWENTY

CELEBRATING VICTORIES, LEARNING FROM LOSSES

In the arena of politics, a realm often characterized by fierce competition and high stakes, the journey is rarely a smooth one. It's a rollercoaster ride of triumphs and setbacks, victories and losses. Both are integral to the political experience, each offering valuable lessons and opportunities for growth. Embracing this duality, learning from both successes and failures, is crucial for any individual or movement seeking to make a lasting impact.

Victories, whether big or small, are milestones that mark progress and affirm the effectiveness of our strategies. They are moments of celebration, a testament to the hard work, dedication, and resilience of those involved. Celebrating victories is not just about reveling in success; it's about acknowledging the collective effort, recognizing individual contributions, and reinforcing the values and principles that underpin the movement.

Celebrating victories can boost morale, strengthen solidarity, and inspire continued action. It can also serve as a powerful recruitment tool, attracting new supporters and energizing existing ones. When we celebrate our wins, we create a positive feedback loop that reinforces our commitment to our cause and fuels our determination to achieve even greater success.

However, it's equally important to learn from our losses. Defeat is not a sign of failure; it's an opportunity for growth and reflection. It's a chance to assess our strategies, identify our weaknesses, and learn from our mistakes. By analyzing what went wrong, we can refine our approach, develop new tactics, and emerge stronger and more resilient.

Learning from losses requires humility, honesty, and a willingness to confront uncomfortable truths. It means acknowledging our shortcomings, taking responsibility for our mistakes, and seeking out feedback from others. It also means being open to new ideas, adapting to changing circumstances, and learning from the experiences of others who have faced similar challenges.

Losses can also be a source of motivation and inspiration. They can ignite a renewed sense of purpose, strengthen our resolve, and galvanize us to action. When we face setbacks, we are often forced to reassess our priorities, re-evaluate our strategies, and recommit to our goals. This process of introspection can lead to greater clarity, focus, and determination.

The ability to learn from losses is a hallmark of great leaders and successful movements. It's a testament to their resilience, adaptability, and commitment to continuous improvement. By embracing failure as a learning opportunity, we can turn setbacks into stepping stones, transforming adversity into advantage.

In the political arena, where the stakes are high and the

consequences of failure can be significant, the ability to learn from losses is particularly crucial. It's what allows us to bounce back from defeat, refine our strategies, and ultimately achieve our goals. It's what enables us to build a movement that is resilient, adaptable, and capable of withstanding the inevitable challenges that come with political engagement.

Celebrating victories and learning from losses are two sides of the same coin. They are both essential components of a healthy and sustainable political movement. By embracing both success and failure, we can create a culture of continuous learning and improvement, one that is driven by a shared commitment to progress and a relentless pursuit of justice.

❦❦❦

"Celebrate your victories, for they are milestones on your journey to greatness. Learn from your losses, for they are the stepping stones that lead to wisdom and growth. Remember, the true measure of a leader is not the number of battles won, but the ability to rise stronger from defeat."

TWENTY-ONE
SUMMARY

The path to political empowerment for women is a multifaceted journey, fraught with challenges and brimming with opportunities. It requires a strategic blend of personal development, community building, and engagement with the political landscape. As we've explored in this book, "She Governs and at the Helm," there are numerous strategies that women can employ to amplify their voices, influence decision-making, and create lasting change.

The foundation of political empowerment lies in finding one's unique political voice. This involves a deep dive into personal values, passions, and the desired impact on the world. It's about recognizing the inherent value of one's perspective and utilizing it as a compass to navigate the complexities of the political arena.

Building strong networks is a cornerstone of political influence. By fostering authentic connections with like-minded individuals and organizations, women can amplify their impact, access valuable resources, and create a collective force for change. These networks provide support, mentorship, and solidarity, empowering women to overcome obstacles and navigate the often-challenging political landscape.

Mastering the art of persuasion and influence is crucial for achieving political goals. Effective communication, tailored messaging, and building trust are key components of this art. By understanding their audience, framing arguments persuasively, and leveraging storytelling techniques, women can inspire action, mobilize support, and drive meaningful change.

Navigating political structures requires a deep understanding of the systems and processes that govern decision-making. By building relationships with key stakeholders, engaging in advocacy and lobbying efforts, and collaborating with diverse groups, women can effectively navigate these structures and influence policy outcomes.

Fundraising is the lifeblood of any political campaign. By developing comprehensive fundraising plans, cultivating relationships with donors, and diversifying funding sources, women can secure the resources needed to run successful campaigns and achieve their political aspirations.

Crafting winning messages is essential for connecting with voters and building a movement for change. A compelling message should resonate with voters' concerns and aspirations, offer a vision for the future, and be consistent across all campaign platforms. By utilizing storytelling, repetition, and humor, women can create messages that are memorable, engaging, and impactful.

Mastering public speaking is a transformative skill for women in politics. It's about connecting with audiences on a deep level, inspiring action, and leaving a lasting impact. By preparing thoroughly, practicing their delivery, and overcoming nervousness, women can become confident and effective communicators who can move hearts and minds.

The media can be both a friend and a foe for women in politics. It can amplify their voices and highlight their achievements, but it can also perpetuate harmful stereotypes and distort their message.

Navigating this complex relationship requires a strategic approach, including building relationships with journalists, crafting compelling narratives, and utilizing social media effectively.

Leading with authenticity is a powerful differentiator for women in politics. It involves being true to oneself, embracing one's values, and leading with integrity. Authentic leadership builds trust, inspires others, and creates a more positive and productive environment.

Overcoming obstacles and biases is a critical challenge for women in politics. By raising awareness, building support networks, developing skills, and advocating for systemic change, women can dismantle these barriers and create a more inclusive and equitable political landscape.

Mentoring the next generation is a legacy-building endeavor. By sharing their knowledge, experience, and wisdom, women leaders can empower young women to reach their full potential and create a more inclusive and representative democracy.

The power of collaboration cannot be overstated in the political realm. By joining forces with other women, grassroots organizations, and diverse stakeholders, women can amplify their impact, achieve greater goals, and build a more sustainable movement for change.

Transitioning from activism to policy requires a strategic shift, focusing on developing a comprehensive policy agenda, engaging with policymakers, and building broad-based support. By effectively advocating for their cause, women can influence policy decisions and create lasting change.

Negotiating the political landscape involves understanding the needs and interests of all parties involved, building relationships, and finding common ground. By mastering the art of negotiation, women can build coalitions, overcome obstacles, and achieve their political goals.

Balancing personal and political life is a constant challenge for women in leadership. By setting clear boundaries, building a strong support system, prioritizing self-care, and communicating openly, women can create a fulfilling and sustainable life that honors both their personal and professional aspirations.

In conclusion, the path to political empowerment for women is a complex and dynamic journey. By embracing these strategies, cultivating resilience, and supporting each other, women can break barriers, redefine leadership, and create a more just and equitable world for all.

ᗞᗞᗞ

Citation And References

This book represents the culmination of extensive research and meticulous analysis, incorporating a diverse range of sources, including numerous books, scholarly studies, and personal experiences. Additionally, I have scoured various websites to gather relevant information and data essential for the compilation of this work. I have taken every precaution to ensure the accuracy of the information presented and have diligently cited all sources to acknowledge their contributions.

Despite these efforts, the possibility of inadvertent errors remains. I deeply value the insights of my readers and appreciate any feedback that can help identify and rectify such inaccuracies. I encourage you to bring any discrepancies to my attention.

Your feedback is not only welcome but crucial, as it will aid in correcting current editions and enhancing the content of future ones. I am committed to maintaining the highest standards of accuracy and reliability in my work and thank you for your support and understanding.

Additionally, I firmly uphold the principle of freedom of speech and expression as guaranteed under Article 19(1)(a) of the Constitution of India, and I respect the diverse viewpoints and expressions of all readers.

ppp

Other Books Of The Author

1. Empowering Minds: A Journey into Women's Self-Discovery and Power
2. The Dynamics of Motivation: Catalyzing Thought into Action
3. Meditation and Mental Well Being: The Path to Inner Peace and Clarity
4. The Psychology of Child Education: Nurturing Future Generations
5. Ethical Enlightenment: A Modern Guide to Living with Integrity
6. Voices of Empowerment: Stories of Women Rising Against Odds
7. Social Psychology in Everyday Life: Understanding Human Connections
8. The Essence of Motivational Speaking: Inspiring Change in Others
9. Balancing Acts: Women, Work, and the Will to Lead
10. Guiding with Grace: Raising Children with Compassion and Awareness
11. The Power of Positive Aging: Embracing Life After Fifty
12. Building Resilient Communities: Social Work in Action
13. The Ethical Educator: Principles for Teaching and Learning
14. From Insight to Impact: Social Psychology for a Better World
15. The Ethics of Empathy: A Guide to Ethical Living
16. The Science of Empowering the Self: Navigating Life's Challenges with Psychological Wisdom
17. The Mindful Conscious Leader: Meditation Techniques for Modern Management
18. Pioneering Spirit: Women's Pathways to Leadership and Empowerment
19. Feeling to Healing: The Role of Emotional Intelligence in Child Development
20. Transformative Talks and Words of Inspiration: Insights into Motivational Oratory

Bhajan

101. Pilgrimage of the Soul: Spiritual Journeys in India

❦❦❦

Contact

Dr. Minakshi Bansal
Social Activist
Ahmedabad, Gujarat, Bharat
minakshiindiag20@yahoo.com

❦❦❦

|| LOKAHA SAMASTHAHA SUKHINO BHAVANTU ||